All rights reserved.

No part of this publication may be reproduced stored in a retrieval system or transmitted, in any form or by any means, electronic, mechanical, photocopying, recording or otherwise, without the prior permission of the publishers.

ISBN No. 0-9537761-0-7

Published by D. K. Beard and D. Mark.

Printed by:
Nelson Press Co. Ltd,
Kingswood Grove, Douglas, Isle of Man, IM1 3LY.

Co-Authors

Derek Mark. Well known Lancashire league all-rounder with Accrington. Dedicated lover of cricket and whole heartedly committed to improving boys, girls, young adults and senior players skill at the game. A coach at King William's College in the Isle of Man for the past twenty years he has produced many fine cricketers and successful teams.

Don Beard. A journeyman cricketer and P.E. teacher who has played cricket at many levels during the last 40 years. He is also a cricket fanatic and has been instrumental in fostering a love of cricket and a keen desire to excel at the game in many pupils both young and old.

Acknowledgements

Mike Haywood, for the time he has given up and the patience he has shown while we discussed the best position for the photographs.

King Williams College, for the use of their facilities.

Nelson Press, Isle of Man, in particular Michael Gilbertson and Mark Adams for their pleasant and cheerful indulgence when we returned with alterations and finicky additions to photographs and diagrams.

Contents

Page

- 1. The Grip
- 2. The Stance
- 17. The Backlift
- 25. The Forward Defensive Stroke
- 37. The Off Drive
- 49. The On Drive
- 55. The Straight Drive
- 58. The Lofted Drive
- 59. The Cover Drive
- 63. The Chassé Drive
- 69. Leg glance off the front foot
- 77. The Sweep
- 83. The Backward Defensive Stroke
- 93. Back foot attacking shot played with a straight bat.
- 97. Leg glance off the back foot
- 105. The Pull to leg off the back foot
- 115. The Hook
- 123. The Square Cut
- 135. The Late Cut
- 139. Left Handed Batsmen
- 140. Equipment

141. In the Practise Net
142. Before Batting
143. Batting
145. Running between Wickets

Glossary

(GL) Good length. A ball that puts the batsman in two minds. Whether to play forward or back.

(OP) Over pitched. A ball that pitches too far up to the batsman.

(SP) Short pitched. A ball that is short of a good length forcing the batsman to play off the back foot.

Ball 'pops'. A ball that lifts off a good length.

Gate. The gap left between a batman's pads and his bat when playing a shot.

Yorker. An over pitched ball that lands near the batman's feet and goes under or into the bottom of his bat.

THE GRIP
(For the Right Handed Batsman)

A correct grip is essential in ensuring that the face of the bat comes down with full contact on the ball.

Fig. 1

Details of the Grip

1. The top hand is situated approximately one inch from the top of the bat handle.

    The 'V' formed by the thumb and forefinger is in a line between the splice and the outside edge of the bat.

2. The bottom hand is placed below the top hand so that the gloves are just touching. The 'V' formed by the thumb and forefinger also points between the splice and the outside edge.

3. The two 'V's' are in line with each other.

4. The back of the top hand should be facing between mid-off and extra cover when in the stance position.

THE GRIP

Fault No. 1

The top hand is behind the handle with the 'V' pointing down the splice.

Fig. 2

This restricts the drive as the arms are made to 'lock-out' and the bat cannot be brought through in the correct manner.

Possible Dismissal

It is likely that, when driving off the front foot, the ball will be hit on the up into the cover area.

Comment

This grip could be used effectively by a batsman who wishes to rely solely on defence.

THE GRIP

Fault No. 2
The right hand is moved round the bat handle towards the right knee.

Fig. 3

This creates an outside to inside movement across the line of the ball.

Possible Dismissal

Any movement in the air or off the seam away from the batsman, i.e. from leg to off, will create problems and could lead to a catch being given in the slip/gully area.

THE GRIP

Fault No. 3

The hands are too far apart – right hand at the bottom of the handle.

Fig. 4

The hands are not able to work as a unit and this will restrict the batsman when he is attempting to drive the ball.

Possible Dismissal

The batsman will tend to hit the ball into the air when driving.

Comment

A batsman with this sort of grip would be inclined to be defensive, with his main scoring shots the pull and the cut.

THE STANCE

The stance must be comfortable and enable the batsman to move easily in any direction.

Fig. 5

Fig. 6

Details of the Stance

1. The feet should be comfortably apart and the weight evenly balanced.

2. The left hand should rest on the left thigh with the left elbow inclined towards the bowler.

3. The toe of the bat should be grounded behind the little toe of the right foot with respect to guard taken.

4. The batsman should be in a sideways-on position and looking over his left shoulder down the pitch.

5. The eyes must remain level.

6. The batsman should focus on the ball as the bowler is running in to bowl, keeping the head perfectly still.

7. As the bowler runs in to bowl the batsman is advised to pat the crease in preparation for the playing of the ball.

THE STANCE

Fault No. 1

The eyes are not level but tilted, with the head leaning to the off-side.

Fig. 7

This creates a lack of balance forcing the front foot to lead to the off-side as the initial movement.

Comment

This is a common fault among many batsmen. A good tip is to advise the batsman to wear a helmet and take up his stance. The grill will then indicate whether his eyes are level.

THE STANCE

Fault No. 2

Too open a stance.

Fig. 8

The batsman could have opened up his stance because he is having difficulty playing the ball on the on-side of the pitch, or in the hope that his leg-side shots will improve. This is probably true, but it could be that he will make himself vulnerable to the away swinger pitched on or outside the off stump.

He will also be caught chest-on when playing off the back foot, thereby hitting across the line of the ball. Any ball moving towards the slips will cause him trouble.

THE STANCE

Fault No. 3

Closed stance. The batsman has his shoulder pointing towards mid-off.

Fig. 9

This position is usually taken by a player who is strong on or outside his off-stump, especially when driving.

Possible Dismissal

The weakness would probably lie on or outside the line of the leg stump.

Any ball pitched up on the leg stump or just outside would create the likelihood of a catch to leg slip or the mid-wicket area.

An LBW decision is also likely to the ball pitching leg or leg and middle.

BACKLIFT

The pick-up of the bat prior to delivery.

Fig. 10

Fig. 11

Details of the Backlift

1. The bat must be lifted straight back towards the middle stump.

2. The left hand must be the controlling hand in order to ensure that the bat comes down straight.

3. The bat must be taken back until the left forearm is parallel to the ground and the toe of the bat is around shoulder height.

4. At this stage the face of the bat opens slightly towards point.

BACKLIFT

Fault No. 1
The bat is picked up towards gully.

Fig. 12

The bat cannot come down straight and two faults can occur from this type of pick-up.

    a) The batsman steers the ball into the cover area.

    b) The batsman hits across the line of the ball.

Possible Dismissal

    a) Catches to cover or behind the wicket on the off-side.

    b) Catches to the wicket-keeper or slips or could be bowled by an in-swinging yorker.

BACKLIFT

Fault No. 2
The bat is picked up towards leg slip.

Fig. 13

The bat comes across the ball from the direction of leg slip towards cover, making it difficult to play any ball on or just outside the leg stump

Possible Dismissal

The batsman is vulnerable to the fast yorker.

BACKLIFT

Fault No. 3

A short, almost non-existent backlift.

Fig. 14

Fig. 15

This is not necessarily a serious fault because some batsmen chose to restrict their backlift when playing against quick bowlers as they do not have the time for a high backlift

This type of batsman usually plays from the crease with very little foot movement, either forward or back. A lot of their scoring shots are nudges behind the wicket. They tend to eliminate the pull shot because it is not possible to hit the ball down with no backlift.

FORWARD DEFENSIVE STROKE

This stroke is played to a good length ball. A ball that has the batsman in two minds – whether to play forward or back.

Fig. 16

Fig. 17

Details of the Forward Defensive Stroke

1. A straight, high pick-up.

2. Head and left shoulder lead onto the line of the ball.

3. A comfortable stride should be made with the front foot, placing the foot as close as possible to the pitch of the ball. (see diagram).

4. The back leg should be straight, as this will position the batsman's head over the ball.

5. The position of the left elbow (fig. 16 or 17) is important in order to maintain the shape of the shot and make sure that the full face of the bat meets the ball.

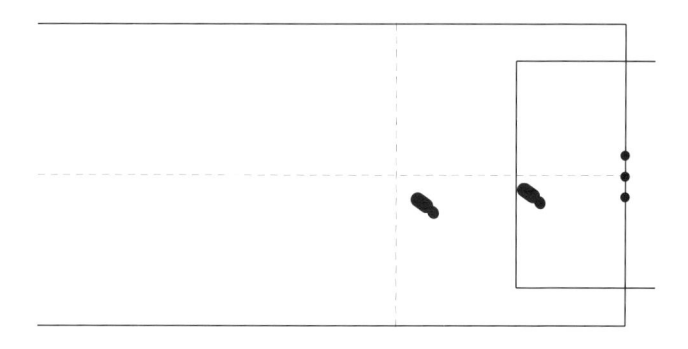

FORWARD DEFENSIVE STROKE

Fault No. 1

The batsman's front foot leads to the on-side of the line of the ball.

Fig. 18

This leaves a gap between bat and pad.

Possible Dismissal

A ball moving from off to leg can go through the gap or 'gate'.

Maybe caught behind from the ball leaving the batsman.

A likelihood of being bowled by a yorker.

FORWARD DEFENSIVE STROKE

Fault No. 2

The batsman's front foot leads to the off-side of the line of the ball.

Fig. 19

The batsman is forced to play around his front pad.

Possible Dismissal

A possible lbw decision from a ball pitched wicket to wicket.

A catch given to silly mid-on, or behind the wicket on the leg side.

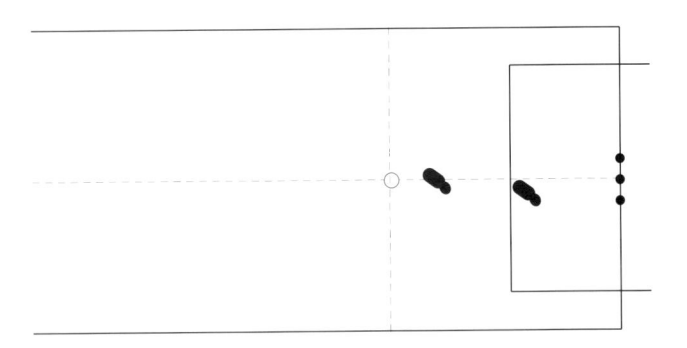

Forward defensive. Foot leading to off-side of ball.

FORWARD DEFENSIVE STROKE
Fault No. 3
The batsman plays with a straight front leg

Fig. 20

This prevents the head and shoulders leading into the line of the ball as the initial movement. The weight distribution is incorrect causing the upper body to lean back, which means that the ball cannot be watched right onto the face of the bat. A gap is also left between bat and pad.

Possible Dismissal

The batsman can be out caught behind as any movement off the pitch will create problems.

He may be bowled through the gap.

FORWARD DEFENSIVE STROKE

Fault No. 4

The front foot does not get close enough to the pitch of the ball.

Fig. 21

The batsman takes a shorter stride than is necessary to get his front foot close to the pitch of the ball. This short stride makes it impossible to control the stroke.

Possible Dismissal

A catch to forward short leg or silly mid-off from the ball that 'pops', or caught behind the wicket off the away swinger.

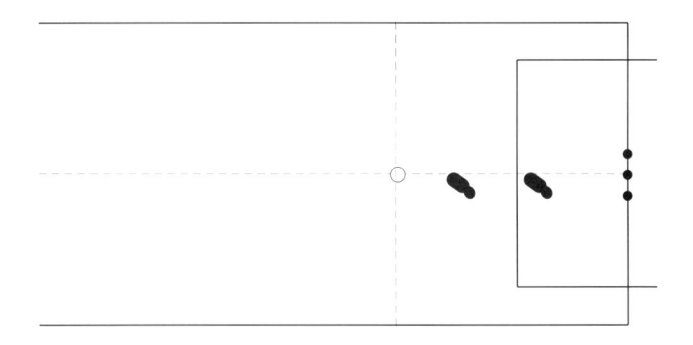

Forward defensive. Short stride.

FORWARD DEFENSIVE STROKE

Fault No. 5

The left elbow loses its required shape by pulling away to the on-side.

Fig. 22

This is a common fault. It enables the right hand to take control and the batsman can easily play across, rather than through, the line of the ball.

Possible Dismissal

A catch may be given to slips or wicket keeper from any ball moving away from the bat.

Comment

It is important for the batsman to control all straight bat shots with his left hand and keep the shape. From a side-on view it can be seen that this shape resembles a figure 9 with the bat as the stem of that figure.

THE OFF-DRIVE

This stroke is played to a ball which is well pitched up, usually of half volley length, on the line or just outside the line of the off stump.

Fig. 23

Details of the Stroke

1. A straight, high pick-up.
2. Head and shoulder lead onto the line of the ball.
3. A comfortable stride should be made with the front foot, placing the foot as close to the pitch of the ball as is possible.
4. The back leg should be straight.
5. The left elbow should be kept high.
6. The shot is an attacking shot and is played vigorously with either a check swing drive or a full follow through.

Comment

A full swing drive is preferable, as when playing the check swing drive more right hand comes into the shot. This forces the head back giving the probability of the ball being hit into the air.

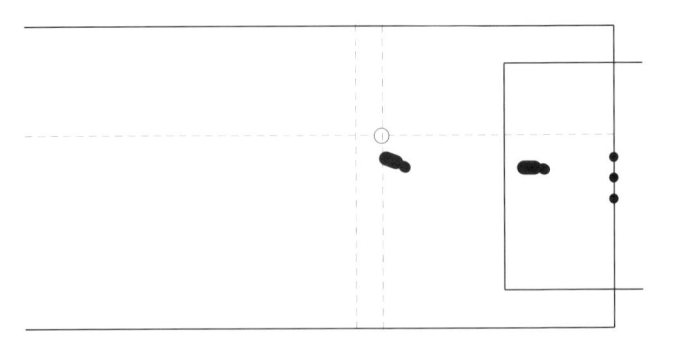

Off drive – correct. Weight distribution as shown.

THE OFF-DRIVE

Fault No. 1

The initial movement is for the batsman's back foot to move outside the leg stump.

Fig. 24

Instead of the front foot travelling down the pitch towards the ball with the head and shoulder leading – it will travel in a direction between point and cover. Therefore the batsman will play across the line of the ball.

Possible Dismissal

An edge to the wicket keeper or slips through being late on the ball or an inside edge onto the stumps.

THE OFF-DRIVE

Fault No. 2
The front foot leads into the shot down the line of the leg or middle stump.

Fig. 25

This batsman automatically leads with his front foot down the line of the middle stump. Therefore any ball pitching on or outside off stump causes him to play away from his pad.

The ball that pitches leg stump or just outside causes him to play round his front pad.

Possible Dismissal

There is a likelihood of catches being given behind the wicket from the ball which moves away. The ball that comes back goes through the gate.

If the ball pitches leg stump then an lbw decision is possible.

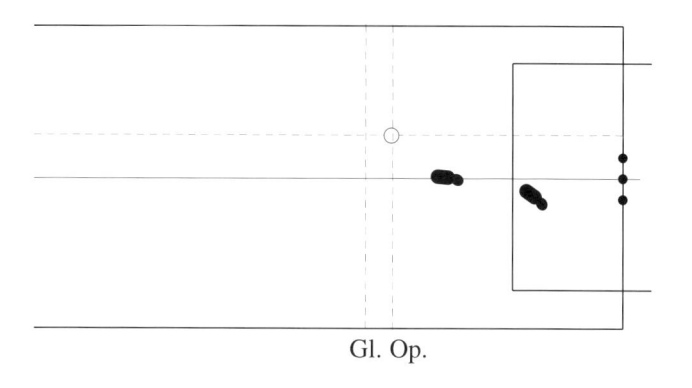

Gl. Op.

Front foot leads down line of middle stump.

THE OFF-DRIVE

Fault No. 3

The batsman does not get his front foot well forward and as close to the pitch of the ball as possible.

Fig. 26

He is unable to drive with his head over the ball. The head stays back and it is therefore impossible to watch the ball onto the bat.

Possible Dismissal

Any movement in the air or off the pitch from the quicker bowlers will cause problems.

Lbw decisions are likely

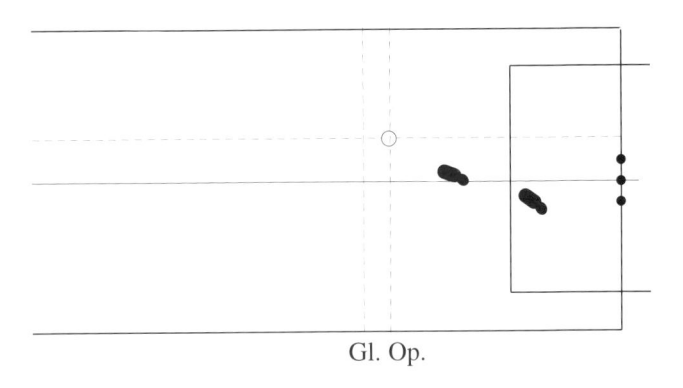

Gl. Op.

Off drive. Batsman plays with a short front foot stride.

THE OFF-DRIVE

Fault No. 4

The batsman's back leg does not remain straight while playing the ball but bends.

Fig. 27

The batman's head is prevented from leading into the ball and he is unable to see the ball onto the face of the bat.

This lean back can cause the ball to be hit into the air.

Possible Dismissal

Any movement in the air will create problems leading to catches behind the wicket.

THE OFF-DRIVE

Fault No. 5

The batsman's left elbow does not retain its shape but drops away.

Fig. 28

The batman loses control of the direction of the shot as he finds it difficult to bring the bat through straight.

His balance is affected.

Possible Dismissal

He is likely to give an outside edge into the slips.

He can be caught at mid-wicket or wide mid-on.

ON DRIVE

This shot is played to the well pitched up ball on the line or just outside the line of the leg stump.

Fig. 29a

Fig. 29b

Details of the Shot

1. High pick-up.
2. The batsman turns his left shoulder slightly towards the line of the ball.
3. The head and shoulders lead towards the ball.
4. The front foot follows with a shorter stride than is used for the off-drive.
5. The front foot should point in the direction of mid-off.
6. The ball is hit just ahead of the front pad.
7. The ball must be allowed to come onto the bat.

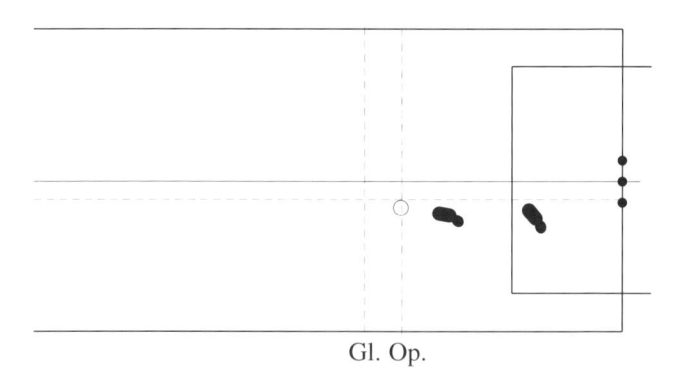

Gl. Op.

On drive – Correct. Slightly shorter stride than off-drive playing ball just in front of the front pad.

ON DRIVE

Fault No. 1

The front foot leads down the line of the middle stump.

Fig. 30

This allows the head to fall to the off-side of the ball. The batsman then loses his balance and he is forced to play around the front pad.

Possible Dismissal

The ball is hit in the air towards mid-wicket.

Possible lbw decision if the ball is missed.

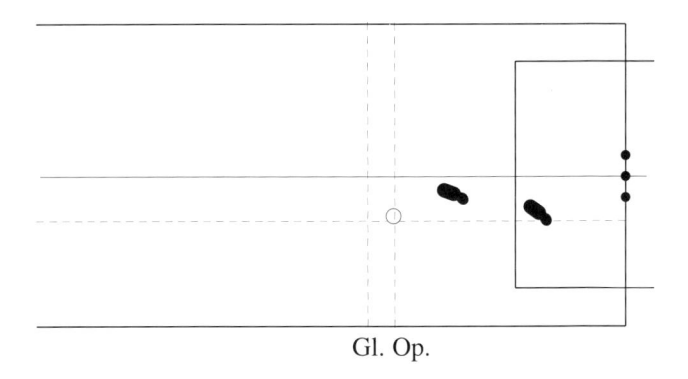

Gl. Op.

On drive. Front foot leading down line of middle stump.

ON DRIVE

Fault No. 2

The batsman points his foot towards mid-on.

Fig. 31

This causes the batsman to play from an open chested position bringing the right side into play and causing a loss of balance.

Possible Dismissal

The ball is hit in the air on the leg side – possible catches in the area from mid-on to mid-wicket

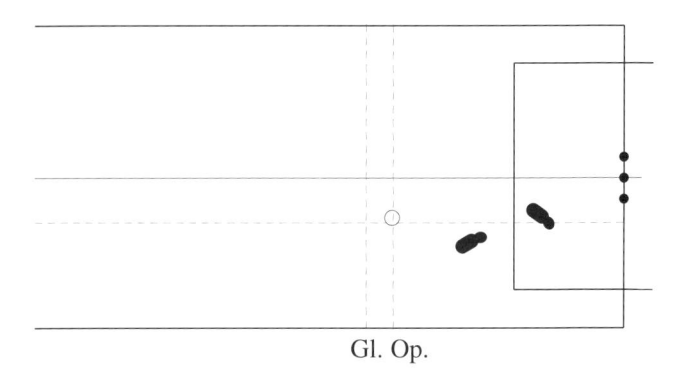

Gl. Op.

On drive. Front foot leading towards mid-on.

THE STRAIGHT DRIVE

This shot is played to a half volley or well pitched-up ball on the stumps.

Fig. 32

Details of the Straight Drive

1. High pick-up.
2. The head and shoulders lead onto the line of the ball.
3. A comfortable stride is made with the front foot, placing the foot as close as possible to the pitch of the ball.
4. The back leg remains straight.
5. The left elbow is kept high in order to maintain the shape of the shot.
6. The ball is played as late as possible giving the batsman time to adjust to any movement in the air or off the pitch.
7. The shot is aimed into the V between mid-off and mid-on.
8. If a lofted drive is required – the ball is met a little earlier in the swing and hit on the up.

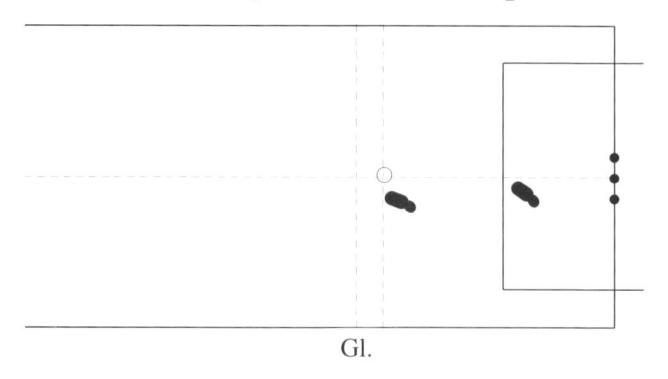

Gl.

Straight drive correct

THE STRAIGHT DRIVE

The faults of the straight drive are the same as for the off-drive.

Fault 1
The initial movement is for the batsman's back foot to move outside the leg stump.

Fault 2
The batsman does not get his front foot well forward and as close to the pitch of the ball as possible.

Fault 3
The batsman's back leg does not remain straight while playing the ball but bends.

Fault 4
The batsman's left elbow does not retain its shape but drops away.

These faults are the same as faults 1, 3, 4, 5 of the off-drive and the dismissal remain the same. Please refer to pages 37-48.

THE LOFTED DRIVE

If the batsman wishes to play a lofted drive then the ball must be taken a little earlier but still hit with a full swing.

Possible Dismissal

Caught at mid-on or mid-off if the shot is checked.

COVER DRIVE

This stroke is played to a ball which is well pitched-up and up to one foot outside the line of the off stump.

Fig. 33

Details of the Cover Drive

1. High pick-up.

2. A turning of the left shoulder towards the ball.

3. Head and shoulder lead onto the line of the ball.

4. The front foot is placed as close to the pitch of the ball as possible.

5. The front foot points to extra cover.

6. The ball is hit vigorously with a full swing or check swing drive.

THE COVER DRIVE

Fault 1

The initial movement is for the batsman's back foot to move outside the leg stump.

Fault 24

The front foot leads into the shot down the line of the middle stump.

Fault 3

The batsman does not get his front foot well forward and as close to the pitch of the ball as possible.

Fault 4

The batsman's back leg does not remain straight while playing the ball but bends.

Fault 5

The batsman's left elbow does not retain its shape but drops away.

These faults are the same as the faults that occur in the off-drive.

Please refer to pages 37-48

THE COVER DRIVE

Fault No. 6
The shot is attempted to a ball which is too wide of the off-stump.

The batsman is forced to play too far away from his front pad, he over-reaches and fails to get any power or direction into the shot.

Possible Dismissal
He can easily get an edge and be caught in the slip or gully area.

Comment
The cover drive is a dangerous shot to play early in the innings when the ball is swinging. A batsman must learn when not to play this shot. If the ball is too wide it should **not** be played at.

Fig. 34

THE CHASSÉ DRIVE
(Lofted and along the ground)

This shot is played to a slow ball when there is very little turn in the pitch.

Fig. 35

Fig. 36

Fig. 37

Details of the Chassé Drive
(Lofted and along the ground)

1. High pick-up.

2. Head and shoulder lead into the line of the ball.

3. The front foot is placed in the correct position (see figure 35).

4. This is followed by the back foot which moves close to and behind the front foot. It remains parallel to the crease ensuring that the batsman remains in a sideways-on position, i.e., looking over his left shoulder at the ball.

5. The front foot, still led by the head and shoulder, then makes a further movement towards the ball as in the straight drive.

6. The ball is hit early, on the up stroke and hit over mid-on or mid-off.

7. The ball is hit late and driven along the ground.

THE CHASSÉ DRIVE

Fault No. 1

Misjudgment of the length of the ball.

Fig. 36

The batsman fails to get into the correct position to hit the ball on the up.

Possible Dismissal

Stumped.

THE CHASSÉ DRIVE

Fault No. 2

Not maintaining a high elbow position.

Fig. 37

This causes the batsman to hit across the line of the ball.

Possible Dismissal

Caught at wide mid-on.

THE LEG GLANCE OFF THE FRONT FOOT

This shot is played to a good length or slightly over-pitched ball on or outside the line of the leg stump.

Fig. 38

Details of the leg glance off the front foot

1. High pick-up.
2. A slight turning of the left shoulder towards the ball.
3. The head and left shoulder lead onto the line of the ball.
4. The front foot follows with the same shorter stride that is used in the on-drive.
5. The ball is played in front of or slightly across the front pad.
6. The left elbow must remain high and the bat straight.
7. The late turning of the wrists deflects the ball behind square.

LEG GLANCE OFF THE FRONT FOOT

Fault No. 1

The stroke is played to a ball that is too wide down the leg side.

Fig. 39

This means that the bat does not remain close to the body and too fine a contact is made.

Possible Dismissal

Catch to the wicket-keeper moving to his left.

LEG GLANCE OFF THE FRONT FOOT

Fault No. 2

The shot is played with a cross bat.

Fig. 40

The left elbow is not kept high but falls away to the leg side. The right hand takes control and the ball is flicked rather than hit.

Possible Dismissal

The ball is flicked into the air towards mid-wicket or could be top edged into the air anywhere behind the wicket.

LEG GLANCE OFF THE FRONT FOOT

Fault No. 3

The batsman overbalances while playing the shot.

Fig. 41

The batsman leads with his front foot, causing his head to lean to the offside of the ball. This causes him to play on the move, falling away from the ball.

Possible Dismissal

He can easily give a catch to the wicket-keeper or be out to a legside stumping as he overbalances.

THE SWEEP

This stroke is usually played to the off spinner pitching on a good length on middle, or on middle and leg stump.

Fig. 42

Fig. 43

Details of the Shot

1. High pick-up is necessary
2. The head and left shoulder lead towards the line of the ball.
3. A comfortable stride is taken on the front foot with the knee bending.
4. The knee of the back leg bends and touches the ground.
5. The shot is played at full stretch of the arms and in front of the pad.
6. The ball is hit a descending blow with a cross bat.
7. The wrists roll over to keep the ball down.
8. The ball is hit with moderate power.

THE SWEEP

Fault No. 1
Little or no pick-up, causing the ball to be hit on the up.

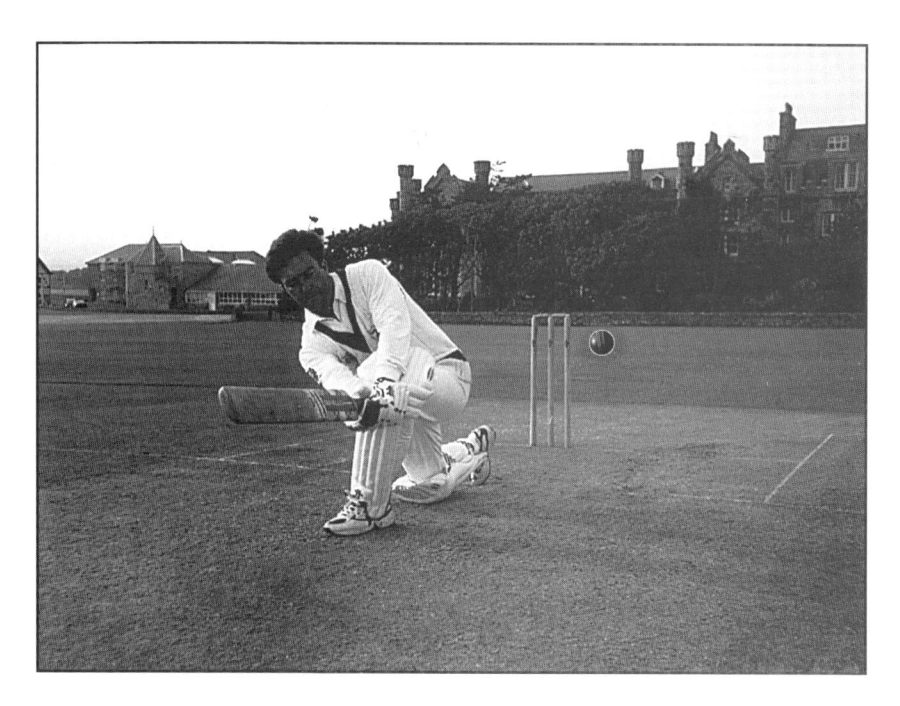

Fig. 44

The batsman is unable to hit the ball down or achieve any power.

Possible Dismissal

The batsman hits the ball in the air. A possible catch to long leg, square leg or mid-wicket.

THE SWEEP

Fault No. 2

The head leads to the off side of the line of the ball.

Fig. 45

The resulting loss of balance means that it is unlikely that the batsman can keep the ball down.

Possible Dismissal
Caught in the area between long leg and mid-wicket.

Comment
The sweep can also be played against the leg spinner or slow left arm orthodox bowler but it is dangerous to do so as the batsman is playing against the spin.

Because the ball is pitching outside the leg stump and the batsman cannot be given out lbw, the pad can be used as a second line of defence.

BACKWARD DEFENSIVE STROKE

This shot is played to a delivery that is just short of a good length on the line of the stumps.

Fig. 46

Fig. 47

Details of the Shot

1. A high straight pick-up.

2. The right foot takes a big stride back parallel to the crease, moving the head onto the line of the ball.

3. This movement is quickly followed by the left foot which also moves back parallel to the crease ensuring that the body is kept in a sideways-on position.

4. The weight of the body is on the back foot with the top half of the body leaning forward.

5. The elbow must remain high (important) with the face of the bat angled to ensure that the shot is played down.

6. The right (bottom) hand is a finger and thumb grip only.

BACKWARD DEFENSIVE STROKE

Fault No. 1

The batsman moves away to square leg in an attempt to play the ball.

Fig. 48

This leaves the stumps uncovered.

Possible Dismissal

(a) An outside edge on to the uncovered stumps (the pads should be used as a second line of defence).

(b) A catch into the slip cordon off an outside edge to the ball moving away off the pitch.

(c) The bowler may sense that the batsman is afraid of being hit and will bowl short and into the body (short legs brought into action).

(d) Any ball moving from off to leg is likely to bowl the batsman between bat and pad.

BACKWARD DEFENSIVE STROKE

Fault No. 2

The batsman does not move his feet parallel to the crease.

Fig. 49

Instead of the batsman's feet being parallel to the crease they move back but point towards cover/extra cover.

He is made to play chest-on to the bowler causing the bat to approach the ball from an outside to inside position.

Possible Dismissal

A result of this could be that any short pitched ball which moves away from the batsman off the pitch creates problems. Possible dismissals are catches given to slips or wicket-keeper.

Lbw to the ball which keeps low.

BACKWARD DEFENSIVE STROKE

Fault No. 3

The batsman fails to get his head behind the line of the ball.

Fig. 50

The batsman does not gets his head behind the line of the ball and plays away from his body, leaving a gap between bat and pad.

Possible Dismissal

Inside edge onto stumps or outside edge to wicket-keeper or slips.

Bowled off the pads or lbw to the ball which keeps low.

BACKWARD DEFENSIVE STROKE

Fault No. 4

The batsman does not keep the top half of his body in a forward poise but leans back.

Fig. 51

Leaning back makes it impossible for the batsman to watch the ball onto the bat. He is unable to angle the bat sufficiently to play the ball down.

Possible Dismissal

He is likely to hit the ball in the air in front of the wicket, therefore giving catches to silly mid-on or silly mid-off.

BACK FOOT ATTACKING SHOT PLAYED WITH A STRAIGHT BAT

This shot is played to a short pitched ball on or outside the line of the stumps, bouncing no higher than the waist.

Fig. 52

Fig. 53

Details of the Stroke

1. A high straight pick-up.

2. The right foot takes a big stride back parallel to the crease moving the head onto the line of the ball.

3. This movement is quickly followed by the left foot which also moves back parallel to the crease keeping the body in a sideways on position.

4. The weight of the body is kept on the back foot with the top half of the body in a forward position.

5. The left elbow must remain high.

6. The ball is hit vigorously with either a full swing or check swing drive.

Comment

The shot is normally played through the V between wide mid-on and wide mid-off. In the main the shot is played with a check swing drive.

As long as the body remains in a forward position it is a safe shot.

Back Foot Attacking Shots. Ball pitching on the stumps. Weight distribution as illustrated.

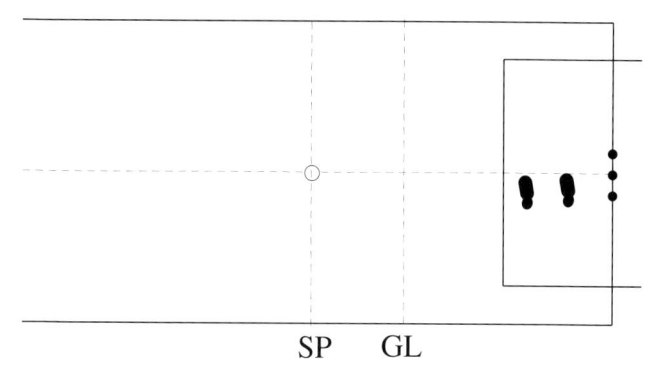

SP   GL

Back Foot Attacking Shots. Short pitched ball on or just outside off stump.

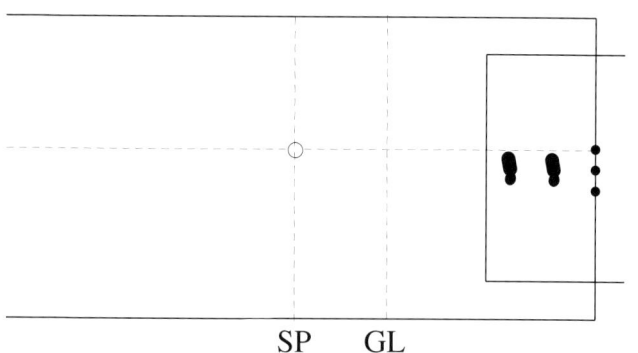

SP   GL

Back Foot Attacking Shots. Short pitched ball on or just outside leg stump. Ball must be played just forward of front pad

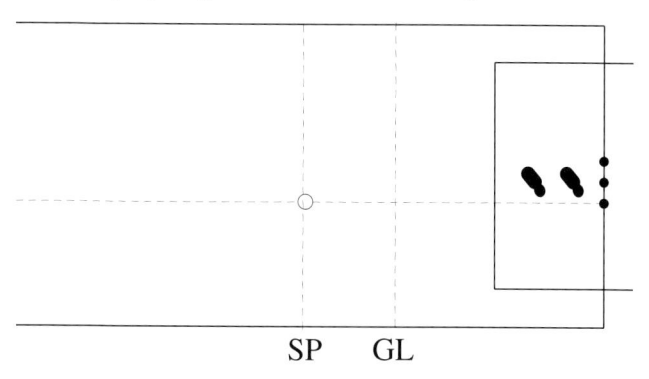

SP   GL

BACK FOOT ATTACKING SHOT FAULTS

Fault No. 1

The batsman moves away to square leg in an attempt to play the shot.

Fault No. 2

The batsman does not move his feet parallel to the crease.

Fault No. 3

The batsman fails to get his head behind the line of the ball.

Fault No. 4

The batsman does not keep the top half of his body in a forward position but leans back.

These faults are the same ones that occur in the back foot defensive stroke and the dismissals remain the same.

Please refer to pages 83-92

LEG GLANCE OFF THE BACK FOOT

This shot is played to a short pitched rising ball on or outside the line of the leg stump.

Fig. 54

Details of the Stroke

1. A high pick-up.
2. The right foot takes a comfortable stride back towards the stumps, keeping the head slightly to the off-side of the line of the ball.
3. The left foot follows the right as in the backward defensive stroke.
4. The main difference is a slight opening of the feet. Instead of remaining parallel to the crease when moving back to the stumps, they must open up to approximately 20° which in effect points them towards cover.
5. The shot must be played just in front of or across the front pad.
6. The left elbow must remain high, ensuring that the bat remains straight.
7. The ball must be allowed to come onto the bat and glance rather than hit.
8. There must be a late turning of the wrists.

Comment
This shot relies upon good timing.

Back Foot Leg Glance – correct
Ball pitching leg stump or just outside.

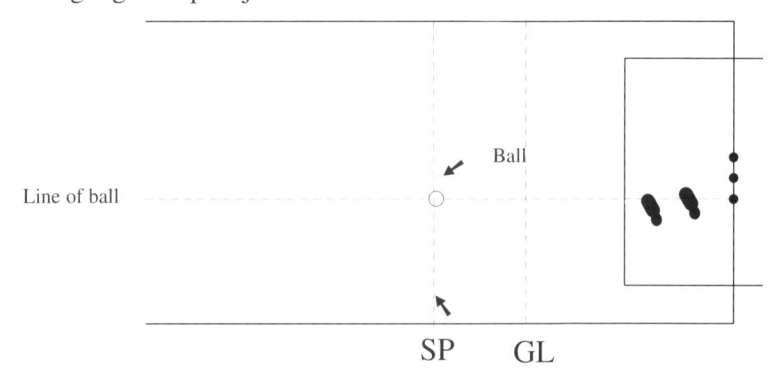

SP   GL

THE LEG GLANCE OFF THE BACK FOOT

Fault No. 1

The stroke is played to a ball that is too wide down the leg side.

Fig. 55

This means that the bat does not remain close to the body and too fine a contact is made.

Possible Dismissal

A catch may be given to the wicket keeper moving to his left.

This fault is the same as for the front foot leg glance.

THE LEG GLANCE OFF THE BACK FOOT

Fault No. 2
The shot is played with a cross bat.

Fig. 56

The left elbow is not kept high but pulls away to the leg side. This means that the right hand takes more control of the shot and the ball is flicked.

Possible Dismissal

The ball is flicked into the air and may be caught behind the wicket in an area between square leg and long leg.

THE LEG GLANCE OFF THE BACK FOOT

Fault No. 3

The batsman moves too far across to the off-side.

Fig. 57

The batsmn gets too far inside the line of the ball and can leave his leg stump uncovered.

Possible Dismissal

He can be bowled leg stump or caught behind the wicket.

Back foot leg glance - incorrect
Feet too far to off-side

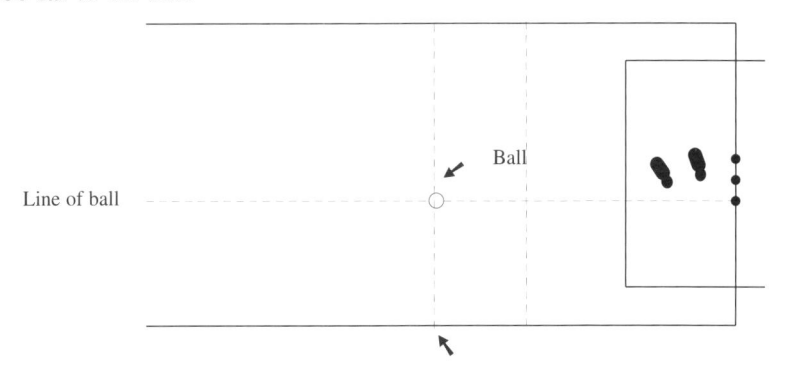

THE PULL TO LEG OFF THE BACK FOOT

This shot is played to a ball that is well short of a good length.

Fig. 58

Fig. 59

Details of the Shot

1. The backlift must be high with the toe of the bat above shoulder height.
2. The back foot must move back and across to the off-side of the line of delivery.
3. The head must be kept still and in line with the ball.
4. The front foot moves back in order to open up the chest and enable the batsman to hit towards mid-wicket.
5. The ball must be played early with the top half of the body in a forward position.
6. The ball must be hit at full stretch of the arms to gain maximum power.
7. At impact the wrists must roll over.
8. There must be a transference of weight from right foot to left foot on completion of the shot.

Pull to leg off back foot. Correct

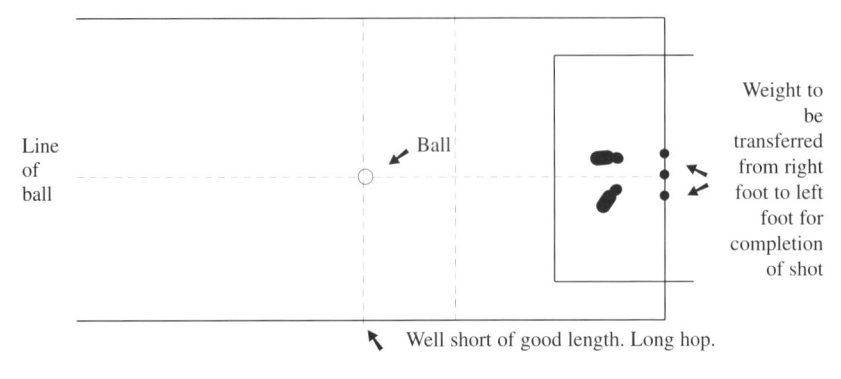

Line of ball

Ball

Weight to be transferred from right foot to left foot for completion of shot

Well short of good length. Long hop.

THE PULL SHOT TO LEG OFF THE BACK FOOT

Fault No. 1
The bat is not picked up high enough.

Fig. 60

The batsman is not able to hit the ball with a descending blow and it is therefore impossible to keep the ball down.

Possible Dismissal

A catch in the direction of backward square leg.

THE PULL SHOT TO LEG OFF THE BACK FOOT

Fault No. 2
The ball is not met early and at full stretch of the arms (but played late, after the ball has been allowed to come onto the batsman)

Fig. 61

The batsman plays the ball too late, which puts him in a cramped position and, results in a weak shot.

Possible Dismissal

A catch in the area of short mid-wicket.

THE PULL SHOT TO LEG OFF THE BACK FOOT

Fault 3

The shot is played too early therefore bringing the head off the line of the ball.

Fig. 62

The shot is likely to be mistimed.

Possible Dismissal

A mishit, with a catch being given in several areas on both sides of the wicket.

THE PULL SHOT TO LEG OFF THE BACK FOOT

Fault 4

The weight is not transferred from right foot to left foot for the completion of the shot

Fig. 63

The weight is not behind the shot and it is difficult to keep the ball down or hit with any power.

Possible Dismissal

The ball is hit in the air behind square leg.

THE HOOK SHOT

This shot is played to a fast, short pitched ball on or outside the leg stump and rising to chest height.

Fig. 64

Details of the Hook Shot

1. High pick-up.

2. The right foot moves back and across bringing the head to the off-side of the line of the ball.

3. The eyes remain fixed on the ball.

4. The body pivots around the right foot.

5. The ball is hit with an ascending bat in a direction between square leg and long leg.

Hook shot. Correct

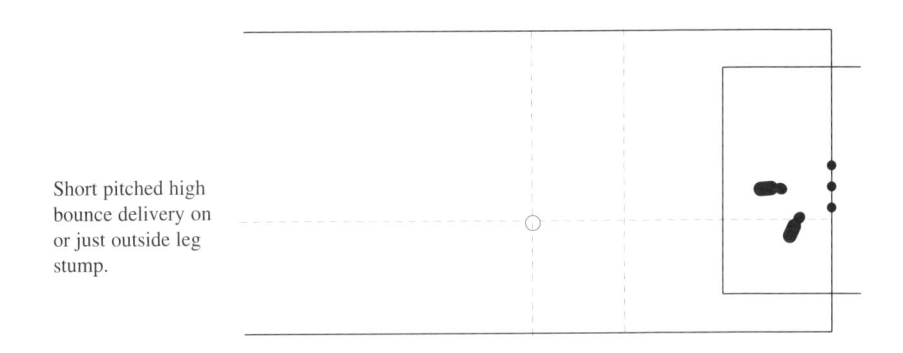

Short pitched high bounce delivery on or just outside leg stump.

THE HOOK

Fault No. 1

The batsman does not move his head to the off-side of the line of the ball.

Fig. 65

The ball is hit in front of the face and any misjudgment can result in injury. The ball is not 'helped' on its way but tends to be hit towards square leg.

Possible Dismissal

The ball is hit into the air with the possible result of a catch at square leg.

THE HOOK

Fault No. 2

The ball is not hit with the arms at full stretch.

Fig. 66

The batsman becomes 'tucked-up' and a weak shot results.

Possible Dismissal

Caught at square leg or fine leg.

Comments

1. It is quite difficult to play a controlled hook.
2. Because this can be a dangerous shot some batsmen tend to duck or sway out of the way of the rising ball.

THE HOOK

Fault No. 3

The batsman backs away to square leg.

Fig. 67

The ball tends to follow the batsman, 'tucks' him up and a weak shot or possible injury is the result.

Possible Dismissal

A top edge to fine leg or square leg.

Hook shot. Incorrect.
Backing away to square leg.

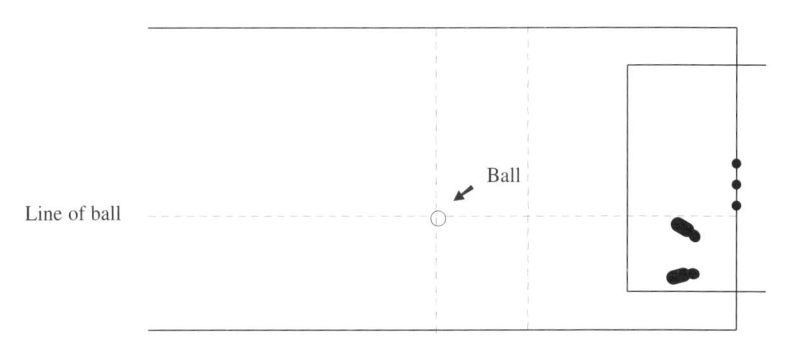

Ball

Line of ball

THE SQUARE CUT

This shot is played to a short pitched ball which passes wide of the off-stump but is within reach and ideally about waist high.

Fig. 68

Details of the Stroke

1. High pick-up.
2. Right foot back and across with the knee bent.
3. Transference of weight to the right foot.
4. The ball hit at full stretch of the arms.
5. The ball hit with a descending bat.
6. The ball watched onto the bat and hit late, either square or just behind.
7. The wrists rolled over on impact to keep the ball down.

Comments

The batsman should have the feeling that his back is towards the bowler as he makes contact.

THE SQUARE CUT

Fault No. 1

Pick up not high enough.

Fig. 69

The batsman is unable to hit the ball down and this can result in a skied shot.

Possible Dismissal

Caught in the third man area.

THE SQUARE CUT

Fault 2

A failure to move the weight to the right foot and bend the knee.

Fig. 70

This causes the batsman to lean away and he loses power in the shot.

Possible Dismissal

Top edge into the slips.

THE SQUARE CUT

Fault 3

The batsman tries to cut the ball that is too close to the off stump.

Fig. 71

The batsman tries to give himself room and compensates by moving his left foot to the on-side. This causes him to lean back when playing the shot.

Possible Dismissal

The shot is mistimed and can result in a catch to the wicket-keeper or slip cordon, or can be played onto the stumps.

Comment
This is a shot quite often seen in one day cricket.

THE SQUARE CUT

Fault 4

The batsman plays the ball from a 'tucked-up' position.

Fig. 72

This fault is often caused by the batsman choosing the wrong ball to square cut. He cannot hit the ball with his arms at full stretch.

Possible Dismissal

Top edge to slips.

THE SQUARE CUT

Fault 5
The back foot goes across the crease rather than back and across.

Fig. 73

The batsman plays the ball too early from a chest-on position and generally hits in front of square. It is difficult for him to get over the ball and he usually hits it in the air.

Possible Dismissal

A catch in the direction of cover.

THE LATE CUT

This shot is played to a ball of good length just outside the off stump.

Fig. 74

Fig. 75

Details of the Stroke

1. High pick-up.
2. The right foot is moved back and across close to the off stump.
3. There must be a transference of weight to the right foot.
4. The ball is hit at full stretch of the arms.
5. The ball is hit a descending blow with the bat.
6. The body is kept low.
7. The ball is hit late, level with or behind the line of the stumps.
8. The wrists roll over to keep the ball down.

FAULTS OF THE LATE CUT

The faults of the late cut are the same as those of the square cut. (Pages 125-128).

Fault 1

Pick up not high enough.

Fault 2

A failure to move the weight to the right foot and bend the knee.

Possible Dismissal

1. Caught in the slips or in the gully.
2. The batsman chops the ball onto his own stumps or hits his own wicket

LEFT HANDED BATSMEN

The actual technique of all the strokes detailed in the book is in essence the same for both right handed and left handed batsmen.

The left handed batsmen, however, are posed problems by certain deliveries.

The first movement of many left handed batsmen is to lead with the front foot to the offside. When the ball is pitched on or just outside the leg stump they are in trouble. The movement is not initiated by the head and right shoulder and as this places the batsmen on the wrong line he tends to overbalance to the off-side. This forces him to flick at the ball which often results in an airborne shot or, if no contact is made, then the ball regularly hits the pad.

Some batsmen find difficulty playing around the leg stump and so compensate by opening up their stance, that is becoming 'chest-on' to the bowler in the hope that it will improve their on-side play.

In some cases this may be true but the batsman becomes more vulnerable outside his off-stump because his foot movement is not sufficient to bring him close enough to the ball which pitched on a good length. The result is often an edged shot.

A good tip for the batsman who does have this trouble with the leg side delivery, is to take a leg stump guard and remain in a sideways position. This will give him more opportunity to play shots to the off-side. There is also less likelihood of an lbw decision against him.

BEFORE BATTING

1. Get ready to bat in good time. There is nothing worse than getting to the wicket flustered after rushing to put on pads, box, thigh pad and adjust helmet straps.

2. Sit outside when you are next man in – it will help you to get used to the light.

3. While you are awaiting your turn to bat observe the bowlers and what they are trying to do with the ball. Also note the field placings, the good and poor fielders and the fast, accurate throwers and whether the fielders in key positions are right or left handed.

4. Walk fairly slowly to the pitch, look around, settle your nerves and concentrate. Loosen up by playing a few practise shots.

5. Do not clutter up your mind by thinking about too many coaching points.

BATTING

1. Do not rush the preliminaries – make sure that you have the correct guard that you want and take your time looking round the field. Be aware of changes in the field placings, especially if they are just for you. They are trying to exploit your weakness or persuade you into making a false shot.

2. Watch every ball carefully and play them on merit. Do not assume the type of ball that is to be bowled next.

3. Take up to five overs to play yourself in.

4. Do not play the ball too early. Lots of batsmen make the mistake of rushing to play the shot and not letting the ball come on to the bat. If played too early the ball is hit slightly on the up which leads to catches.

5. Play shots in the V at the start of your innings. Get used to the light, the bowling, the pace of the pitch and the bounce of the ball before you attempt to cut, pull or hook.

6. If a ball is wide early on in your innings – leave it.

7. When facing a fast bowler who is bowling a little short, think back foot.

8. Treat full tosses with respect. Just try to hit them sensibly into the gaps in the field. Too many players see an easy four runs and try to hit the ball to the boundary, often with a cross bat.

9. Do not allow comments from bowler, fielders or wicket-keeper (known as sledging) or the crowd, to affect your concentration or force you to throw your wicket away.

10. You do not always have to hit the ball hard to score runs. If the bowling is quick and the outfield fast just lean into the ball and push it into the gaps, or using the bowlers' pace, deflect it behind the wicket.

RUNNING BETWEEN WICKETS

1. Good running between wickets is a skill in its own right and of the utmost importance to every young aspiring batsman.

2. Call loudly and firmly.
   Either – Yes, No, or Wait.

3. When backing-up at the non-strikers end keep your bat behind the crease until the ball has left the bowlers hand.

   Then walk forward, but be prepared to ground your bat behind the batting crease if the ball is driven straight back down the pitch.

4. When taking a quick run always ground your bat by stretching your arm out in front of you. Get the maximum amount of extension possible while running as fast as you can.

5. Ground your bat and look for a second run. Try not to run too far past the stumps. Keep your eye on the ball as you turn.

6. Always be prepared for that extra run if the ball is missed by a fielder or thrown in wildly.

7. Do not run on a misfield unless the run is an absolute certainty. The fielder can very quickly have the ball under control.

8. When running, run wide of the pitch – not on it.

9. If the runs are coming slowly look for the quick singles by placement.

10. The extremely short single, i.e., when the ball is dropped at the batsman's feet, should only be taken after discussion with your batting partner.

Equipment

1. Always try to get the best equipment and clothing because if you dress the part you will feel good and this can only improve your attitude towards the discipline needed to become a good cricketer.

2. A helmet is a good idea. Apart from the obvious safety angle it is especially good for batsmen who are in the habit of leaning over and not keeping the eyes level. As soon as a batsman takes up his stance the grill on the helmet will tell him whether or not his head is up and his eyes level.

   The helmet helps to give confidence when leading into a shot with the head and shoulder, especially on poor wickets.

In the Practise Nets

1. Do practise as often as you can.

2. When having net practise always play as though you are in a match situation.

3. Relax and concentrate on each ball bowled. Practise watching the ball closely in the bowlers hand as he moves in to bowl and try to see what it is that he is doing with his fingers and wrist at the time of delivery. If you can, observe the rotation of the seam on its way to you.

4. It is a good idea to practise back foot shoots only for ten minutes each session. whatever the length of the ball may be. Try to watch the ball right onto the bat. All the greatest players are good off the back foot.

5. To improve your powers of concentration get a friend to stand behind the net and chat to you and move around while you are batting. Attempt to shut out the noise and the interference and in doing so you will improve your powers of concentration. Total concentration is very necessary if you are to play a long innings.

6. Practise your all round game. Do not just work on your weak areas. Working on weak areas and not doing particularly well can cause a loss of confidence.